SEVEN
Words
of
Christmas

Also by Robert Morris

Beyond Blessed

Daily Readings from Beyond Blessed

Take the Day Off

ROBERT MORRIS

SEVEN

Words

of

Christmas

THE JOYFUL PROPHECIES
THAT CHANGED THE WORLD

FaithWords

New York • Nashville

FaithWords
Hachette Book Group
1290 Avenue of the Americas, New York, NY 10104
faithwords.com
twitter.com/faithwords

First Edition: October 2020

FaithWords is a division of Hachette Book Group, Inc. The FaithWords name and logo are trademarks of Hachette Book Group, Inc.

The publisher is not responsible for websites (or their content) that are not owned by the publisher.

The Hachette Speakers Bureau provides a wide range of authors for speaking events. To find out more, go to www.hachettespeakersbureau.com or call (866) 376-6591.

All Scripture quotations, unless otherwise indicated, are from the New King James Version®. Copyright © 1982 by Thomas Nelson. Used by permission. All rights reserved.

Scripture quotations marked (NLT) are from the Holy Bible, New Living Translation, copyright © 1996, 2004, 2015 by Tyndale House Foundation. Used by permission of Tyndale House Publishers, a Division of Tyndale House Ministries, Carol Stream, Illinois 60188. All rights reserved.

Print book interior design by Bart Dawson

Library of Congress Cataloging-in-Publication Data
Names: Morris, Robert (Robert Preston), 1961- author.
Title: Seven words of Christmas : the joyful prophecies that changed the world / Robert Morris.
Description: First edition. | Nashville : FaithWords, 2020.
Identifiers: LCCN 2020014849 | ISBN 9781546017295 (hardcover) | ISBN 9781546014942 (ebook)
Subjects: LCSH: Jesus Christ—Nativity. | Jesus Christ—Nativity—Biblical teaching. | Christmas—Biblical teaching. | Christmas.
Classification: LCC BT315.3 .M675 2020 | DDC 232.92—dc23
LC record available at https://lccn.loc.gov/2020014849

ISBNs: 978-1-5460-1729-5 (hardcover), 978-1-5460-1494-2 (ebook)

Printed in Canada

FRI

10 9 8 7 6 5 4 3 2 1

thanks be to God for His indescribable gift!

2 CORINTHIANS 9:15 NKJV

Contents

Guidance

Joy

Redemption

Peace

START HERE!

"Congratulations, Robert. It's a healthy boy. You're a father."

The doctor charged with delivering our first son was looking at me with a big smile on his face and holding a greasy, wriggling, crying, little thing still attached to my wife by an umbilical cord.

In a moment already overflowing with joy, wonder, relief, and exhaustion, the implications of one word entered my ears, broke through my cluttered mind, and triggered an earthquake in my heart.

A *father*?

That moment drew an invisible line through the timeline of my life. On one side of that line I had been many things—a son, a friend, a student (a poor one!), a sinner, and a husband. On the other side, I was a father, and nothing would ever change that. From that moment forward, even if I lived to be 120, I would never, ever *not* be a dad.

What a difference a word can make. Two little syllables can change your life and set you on a whole new path. One solitary word can transform not only how you see yourself but how you see everything else.

How much more significant is it when that word

comes from God Himself? God spoke and the whole universe came into existence. But our wonderful heavenly Father doesn't ordinarily speak in an audible voice. Throughout most of redemptive history, He has spoken through people.

When God speaks through an individual, and He frequently does, we call that a prophecy or a prophetic word. The Bible is filled with them. Throughout the Scriptures God delivered a word to announce His will, His plans, or His heart. And because He is good, His will, plans, and heart are always good. Always redemptive.

So, it shouldn't surprise us to discover that God spoke prophetically through people when it came to bringing about the most important event of all in His

3

grand plan to redeem a big world filled with fallen and broken people. That event was the birth of His only begotten Son, Jesus.

Several years ago, when I began to study the "Christmas story" as told in the opening chapters of Matthew and Luke, I discovered that God delivered seven key prophetic words around the birth of His Son. As a student of the Bible, it didn't surprise me to find seven. It fits one of the most prominent patterns in Scripture.

Through the Bible, the number seven appears repeatedly to signify "completeness" or "perfection." From the seven days of creation on the opening pages of Genesis; to the seven golden lampstands and seven bowls of divine judgment in the book of Revelation;

4

and in every book in between, the number seemingly pops up everywhere.

Is it any wonder God heralded the entry of His Son into the world with seven unique prophetic words?

Please don't miss out on the amazing truth that these words are very much the God of the Universe speaking. Let that sink in. Soak in the majesty and mystery of it. The Lord and King of heaven and earth announces what He is doing to regular Joes and Joannes like you and me.

Seven times God spoke through someone in connection with the birth of His beloved Son. Don't you think we should give an ear to those words? Don't you think we might find some wisdom, some encouragement, some comfort, or some direction in them? Indeed, we will.

You may want to read this book all in one sitting. I've kept it brief enough to make that possible. But I have also divided our exploration of these seven momentous Christmas words into twenty-one bite-sized bits that you can savor and ponder over the course of twenty-one days if you choose.

Indeed, I suggest you use this as an advent season devotional—by yourself or as a family—beginning on December third or fourth, and counting the days to Christmas with a chapter each day.

In each of the seven sections that follow, we will explore one of those glorious prophetic words. In each, there is a single word that jumped out at me, which serves as the heading for that section.

Salvation, Favor, Blessed, Guidance, Joy, Redemption, and Peace. These are good words. Words that describe things that you would love to have a greater abundance of in your life and home.

These are the Seven Words of Christmas. Let's explore them together.

Salvation

Now his father Zacharias was filled
with the Holy Spirit, and prophesied, saying:
"Blessed is the Lord God of Israel,
For He has visited and redeemed His people,
And has raised **up** a horn of salvation for us
In **the** house of His servant David."

LUKE 1:67–69

DAY ONE

*T*he Christmas story begins with a miraculous pregnancy, but not the one that probably jumped to mind when you read those words.

No, our journey through the first word of Christmas begins with an elderly couple living roughly nineteen miles south of Jerusalem, in Hebron—an ancient village nestled in the craggy Judean hills. We begin with Zacharias and Elizabeth; both of the priestly tribe of Levi and direct descendants of Aaron, the first High Priest of Israel.

Although tiny, Hebron looms large in the Old Testament story. In fact, few towns in Israel figure more prominently in Israel's history. One thousand years before Zacharias and Elizabeth lived there, God specifically directed David to go there to be anointed King of Judah following the death of Saul (see 2 Sam. 2:1). David ruled from Hebron for several years before relocating the seat of his kingdom to Jerusalem.

Five centuries before David's time, giants had roamed the hills around their hometown. Reports of these mighty men of great size—the "sons of Anak"—brought back by spies scouting out the land, paralyzed the Israelites with terror as they prepared to enter into the land of promise. But two key Israelite leaders, Joshua and Caleb, hadn't been moved by the reports of these fierce, oversized enemies.

Ultimately, Caleb and his clan conquered this territory, drove out the Canaanite inhabitants (including its giants), and settled here. Faithful Caleb, in obedience to the Lord's specific instructions handed down through Moses, set aside a portion of his territory as a habitation for the Levites—the priestly tribe. This is how, fifteen hundred years later, these two married but childless descendants of Aaron—Zacharias and Elizabeth—came to be living in this remote part of the world during the reign of Caesar Augustus.

As a Levitical priest, Zacharias was required to make regular journeys to Jerusalem whenever it was his turn to administer the temple sacrifices and offerings for a week, as well as during all the great feasts and festivals of the Jewish people.

Zacharias and Elizabeth had lived long and well, yet also carried a lifelong, seemingly unhealable heartache. Luke's gospel makes this plain when he says of this couple:

14

> And they were both righteous before God, walking in all the commandments and ordinances of the Lord blameless. But they had no child, because Elizabeth was barren, and they were both well advanced in years. (Luke 1:6–7)

To be childless in that time and culture was

both humiliating for the couple and economically catastrophic for the wife. Children were viewed as a blessing and therefore evidence of God's favor. What's more, because women usually did not own property or handle money, childless women were often left destitute and reduced to depending solely upon charity when their husbands passed away.

In other words, Zacharias and Elizabeth had a giant in their lives that, despite their faithfulness, had never been slain. But all of that was about to change with the arrival of a startling word from God.

DAY TWO

✳

*Y*ears after the incident, Zacharias could still describe the exact spot where the angel was standing when he delivered the shocking news. In recounting his story to Luke, Zacharias revealed that God's heavenly messenger had suddenly appeared "standing on the right side of the altar of incense" (Luke 1:11).

The altar of incense in the Jerusalem temple was a special place, located just outside of the Holy of Holies, in a chamber called the Holy Place. It was a square pillar overlaid with pure gold and topped with a bowl that held hot coals. There, at sunrise and sunset each day, a priest, chosen by lot, would enter this sacred space alone and offer a very distinct type of incense as an offering to God.

Each morning and evening, hundreds or even thousands of pious Jews would gather in the courts outside to pray as this ceremony took place within, hoping that the offered incense would help carry their petitions up to heaven's throne room.

The week arrived when it was time for Zacharias'

group of priests to minister in the magnificent temple in Jerusalem. On this momentous day, the Lord, through the casting of lots, had chosen Zacharias for the honor of presenting the incense offering.

There, in the second-most sacred space in all of Judaism, Zacharias is startled to see an angel standing beside the altar. This isn't just any angel. It is Gabriel, the "archangel," God's designated messenger for announcements concerning the coming of the Messiah. It was this same Gabriel who, centuries earlier, had appeared to Daniel to explain the strange visions he'd seen. A few months after this appearance to Zacharias, Gabriel will pay a visit a young woman named Mary to give her some surprising news, as well.

The altar of incense is about prayer, and Gabriel's

message on this day is concerning the one prayer
Zacharias and his wife had prayed more than any other
throughout their lives together:

> "Do not be afraid, Zacharias, for your prayer is
> heard; and your wife Elizabeth will bear you a son,
> and you shall call his name John." (Luke 1:13)

19

As if this weren't already enough of a bombshell
announcement, the angel went on to let the old
priest know that this miracle son would grow up to
be the special forerunner of the Messiah, prophesied
by the prophet Malachi in the final words of the Old
Testament. Clearly, this was a lot to take in. When
Zacharias recovered enough to muster a response, it

was not exactly filled with faith and confidence. He replied:

> "How shall I know this? For I am an old man, and my wife is well advanced in years." (Luke 1:18)

I'm not sure you or I would have done any better in those circumstances. But let's give Zacharias credit for one thing. Even in the extreme surprise and disorientation of that moment, he had the presence of mind to choose his words wisely when referring to his wife's age. Whereas he described himself as "an old man," his lovely wife Elizabeth was merely "well advanced in years." Smart man.

Nevertheless, Gabriel wasn't pleased with the old

priest's request for some sort of sign. Apparently when God's top messenger goes to all the trouble to appear to you, he expects you to believe what he tells you:

> And the angel answered and said to him, "I am Gabriel, who stands in the presence of God, and was sent to speak to you and bring you these glad tidings. But behold, you will be mute and not able to speak until the day these things take place, because you did not believe my words which will be fulfilled in their own time." (Luke 1:19–20)

Be careful what you ask for. "Here's a sign for you, Zacharias—not being able to talk." Now, after presenting the incense offering, the performing priest is supposed to walk back out to the outer court and speak a blessing over the pray-ers assembled there. On this day, the congregation sees an elderly priest stagger out from behind the curtains gesturing wildly and pointing back to the Holy Place. He speaks no blessing. He can't. But he has just had an amazing blessing spoken over him.

22

I wonder how many times you and I have frustrated the Lord by greeting one of His wonderful promises or sweet reassurances with skepticism rather than belief. For as we are about to see, our patient, merciful God is faithful to perform His Word.

DAY THREE

I would love to have witnessed the crazy game of charades Zacharias must have played with his wife when he returned home to Hebron and to his waiting wife, Elizabeth. No doubt he tried to use hand gestures and pantomime to describe the encounter he'd had, the message he'd received, and the reason he could no longer speak.

We do know that he took the angel's promise

seriously because the Bible tells us, "Now after those days his wife Elizabeth conceived" (Luke 1:24). In other words, Zacharias did his part!

You'll recall that the angelic message specifically said the child's name was to be John. Zacharias must have communicated that to Elizabeth, because eight days after the birth, on the day the baby boy was to be circumcised, their relatives asked the question all relatives ask brand-new parents. "What's his name?"

Normally in that culture, that question would be answered by the child's father, but Zacharias was still mute at this point, even though the angel's promise had indeed been fulfilled. So, Elizabeth answered instead, telling the well-wishers: "He shall be called John" (Luke 1:60).

24

Their friends and relatives were puzzled by this. They had assumed the boy would be named after his father. Someone pointed out that no one in their extended family or lineage was named John. This seemed like a strange choice. So, they all looked in the direction of the father for confirmation. Zacharias responded by grabbing a tablet and writing emphatically, "His name is John" (Luke 1:63).

As soon as he wrote those words, he was able to speak again. This final act of obedience to the word that had come through the angel set him free. At the very same time, the presence of the Holy Spirit fell upon the new father and, like an Old Testament prophet, he began to prophesy. We won't explore all two-hundred-plus words of what the Spirit of the Lord spoke through Zacharias here. We'll focus on just a few lines. His prophetic word begins with:

> Blessed is the Lord God of Israel, for He has visited and redeemed His people, and has raised up a horn of salvation for us in the house of His servant David. (Luke 1:68–69)

26

A horn of salvation! The Greek word that is translated as "salvation" here is *soteria*, and it carries various meanings, including "deliverance," "preservation," "restoration," and "safety."

It's important to note that this "horn of salvation" Zacharias is prophesying about here is not his son, John. By the Holy Spirit, he is speaking of the one for whom John will one day prepare the way. Gabriel had told Zacharias that his miracle child will be the "forerunner" prophesied by Malachi.

How can we be sure that Zacharias isn't referring to John? Because that horn was rising "in the house of His servant David." Zacharias, as a Levite, was of the house of Levi. Who was a descendant of David? Jesus!

Of course, "Jesus" is merely the Greek-ified version of Jesus' Hebrew name—Yeshua. That, in turn, was a variant of the Old Testament name that reads in our English Bibles as Joshua.

Many people are unaware that the Joshua who served as Moses' military commander and successor was born with a different name. He was originally called Hoshea, which means "salvation." But in

Numbers 13, we see that Moses changed his name to Je-shua, which literally means "Jehovah saves."

This helps us understand why, as we'll learn in an upcoming chapter, Gabriel directed Mary to name her promised miracle baby Jesus.

Salvation is a key message of Christmas because it is, at its heart, the story of God sending His Son to save us from our sin. This is who Jesus is. He is deliverance, preservation, restoration, and safety sent from God! As you move through the busy, often stressful, Christmas season, please don't lose sight of this wonderful truth.

The first word of Christmas is *salvation*!

Favor

Then the angel said to her,
"Do not be afraid, Mary, for you
have found favor with God."

LUKE 1:30

DAY FOUR

✳

*H*eaven's most important messenger has been
sent directly from the most powerful throne
in the universe to deliver the most significant news
any human being has ever received…to a poor girl in
a backwater village in the troubled outer edge of the
Roman Empire.

On this day, roughly six months after visiting
Zacharias beside the altar of incense, the archangel

Gabriel heads for the town of Nazareth in Galilee to tell a startled young girl she will soon become the mother of the Redeemer of the whole world. She's not even married yet, but she's about to get the news that her firstborn will be the "Last Adam," who will make right everything the original Adam made wrong.

Isaiah had foreseen this event more than seven hundred years earlier. "Behold, the virgin shall conceive and bear a Son," he wrote, "and shall call His name Immanuel" (Isa. 7:14). The prophet had peered down through the centuries and saw a day in which a teenage girl who had never known a man would miraculously find herself carrying the child who would literally be "God with us."

Upon arrival, Gabriel's message begins with a

32

remarkable greeting, "Rejoice, highly favored *one*, the Lord *is* with you; blessed *are* you among women!" (Luke 1:28).

"Highly favored"? Why? If they could see this event taking place, the scholars, lawyers, and learned rabbis down in Jerusalem would be bewildered by the selection of *this* girl for such a visit. And they would be stunned by the angelic pronouncement that she, among earth's millions, is the object of God's divine favor.

33

She has no credentials. No one who matters has ever heard of her or her parents. And she's from the wrong end of the country. In this era, the urbanized citizens of Jerusalem tend to view rural Galilee pretty much the same way some people in New York and

Boston view the residents of small West Virginia towns. Hillbillies. Country bumpkins. The Galileans even have a funny accent that gives them away as uneducated rubes.

And yet here the archangel of the Most High stands, telling an openmouthed young lady that she is "highly favored" and "blessed among all women."

34

Mary's response to the angel's greeting is pretty much what you'd expect. She's startled, alarmed, fascinated, and confused—all at the same time. She wonders what the messenger could possibly mean by addressing her with those terms. *Maybe he's at the wrong house?* Gabriel, perceiving her questions reassures her, calling her by name:

"Do not be afraid, Mary, for you have found favor with God." (Luke 1:30)

There's that word again. *Favor.* It's clearly an important one to God. Perhaps we need to know more about that word.

In the meantime, please know that you and I have something in common with that Galilean girl. We're not credentialed either. At least not in any way that matters in the eternal scheme of things, no matter how many degrees, certifications, and awards we may have. Yet, as we're about to see, we too have been highly favored. We too have been invited to participate in God's glorious plan for saving the world.

DAY FIVE

*H*ave you ever had a bombshell of news dropped on you—utterly out of the blue? Most of us have. But no person in the history of the world has ever received news more unexpected or mind-blowing than the message Mary heard from a heavenly herald one evening:

"Do not be afraid, Mary, for you have found favor

with God. And behold, you will conceive in your womb and bring forth a Son, and shall call His name JESUS. He will be great, and will be called the Son of the Highest; and the Lord God will give Him the throne of His father David. And He will reign over the house of Jacob forever, and of His kingdom there will be no end." (Luke 1:30–33)

Mary is no learned rabbi, but the implications of these words are quite clear to her, just as they would have been to any devout Jewish person of that day.

God's messenger has just told her that she's going to give birth to the long-awaited Redeemer-Deliverer of Israel. She recognizes the words, "Son of the Highest" as referring to the Messiah. She recognizes the phrases "of His kingdom there will be no end" and "upon the throne of His father David" as both coming from Isaiah's prophecy of the future Messiah. The very prophecy that says the Messiah will emerge "in Galilee of the Gentiles" (Isa. 9:1).

What a message for a young girl to absorb and process. But there's something else I want you to notice about this angelic message. For a second time in the early moments of this encounter, the angel declares that Mary has "found favor with God." We think we know what this word means.

In my experience, most of us have a concept of favor that involves someone in authority recognizing our good qualities. In other words, we think favor is a reward that we, in some way, have earned or merited. Here's how we tend to think of it. When you're applying for a job and your résumé is one of fifty sitting in a stack on the decision-maker's desk, you hope that your résumé will grab their attention because you know you're a great fit for the position and you'll do a great job. The challenge is getting the opportunity to demonstrate that. So, you pray for "favor."

Make no mistake about it, there is a kind of blessing from heaven that does cause you to stand out in a crowd. The blessing of the Lord can and does cause people to view you favorably, but that is not the meaning of the word Gabriel spoke to Mary.

Luke wrote in Greek—an extremely precise language. And the English word translated as "favor" in Luke 1:30 is the Greek word *charis*. This word appears

136 times in your New Testament, which tells us that it is a very important concept in the New Covenant God established through Jesus' death and resurrection. Yet only six times is it translated as "favor."

The other 130 times *charis* is translated "grace." This is because deeply rooted in the meaning of *charis* is the concept of a "gift"—something wonderful that is utterly free and unearned. It's no accident the average Christian on the street will tell you that the official definition of *grace* is "*unmerited* favor."

As we're about to see, the story of Christmas is the story of the greatest gift ever given. And on this night, Mary has been informed that she has been chosen to literally *deliver* that gift to the world. Highly favored indeed.

40

DAY SIX

*O*ver the last few years, my wife, Debbie, and I have discovered the joys of being grandparents. It's truly the best thing ever. If you follow me on social media, you already know that I'm constantly doting on my growing clan of "grands."

I jokingly say that grandchildren are the only people you're thrilled to see come and relieved to see go (but only because you're exhausted). Parenting is definitely a younger person's game.

The person in charge of decorating our church for the holidays once asked me, "What are your favorite Christmas lights?" I said, "The taillights when everybody goes home." Again, I'm joking! Debbie and I have discovered that having our family around us is one of the greatest joys of this season of life.

I've also been asked if I have a favorite grandchild. In one sense, the answer is, "Whichever one I'm with!" In another sense, I could truthfully say, "They're all my favorite." And it's true. I've discovered that it's possible to have more than one favorite.

As we explore the Seven Words of Christmas, a key truth is already emerging. If you were the only lost and broken person on earth, He would have still sent His only Son to bring you the first word—

42

salvation. And this second word reveals that you are God's favorite. In a miracle that only an all-knowing, all-powerful, all-loving God could pull off, we are *all* His favorites. We are all the focus of His amazing grace.

The only remaining question is whether or not this *charis* gift will be received. Will His message of grace to you be met with belief as it was in Mary?

When she was told the astonishing news of God's favor upon her, she had only one question. "How can this be, since I do not know a man?" (Luke 1:34). Note that she asked "how" not "whether." In other words, she didn't doubt that what the angel had spoken would take place. She only wondered *how* it would happen, given that she was an unmarried virgin.

43

The angel responded by explaining how such a thing could take place:

And the angel answered and said to her, "*The* Holy Spirit will come upon you, and the power of the Highest will overshadow you; therefore, also, that Holy One who is to be born will be called the Son of God. Now indeed, Elizabeth your relative has also conceived a son in her old age; and this is now the sixth month for her who was called barren. For with God nothing will be impossible." (Luke 1:35–37)

God is so gracious. To assure her the angel also lets Mary know that miraculous pregnancies are going around in this historic, momentous moment in time.

44

Her response is one of faith and complete willingness to partner with God in accomplishing His plans and purposes on earth:

> Then Mary said, "Behold the maidservant of the Lord! Let it be to me according to your word." (Luke 1:38)

45

In other words, "Okay! I'm your girl! I wholeheartedly receive whatever it is You want to do through me, Lord!"

God wants to partner with you, too. God spoke this clearly through the birth of His Son. He spoke salvation. And then He spoke grace. This is the season of grace. And that means you're one of God's *favor*ites.

Blessed

...and Elizabeth was filled with the Holy Spirit.
Then she spoke out with a loud voice and said,
"Blessed are you among women,
and blessed is the fruit of your womb!"

LUKE 1:41–42

DAY SEVEN

hen Jesus meets His cousin John the Baptist
for the first time, they are both still being
carried within their mothers' wombs.

Two, related women—one only a teen and the
other well advanced in years—find themselves
eternally linked together in the greatest story ever told.
Both pregnancies have been preceded by a visitation
from the archangel Gabriel. Both are miraculous, but

in different ways and degrees. Both unborn children had been foretold in Old Testament prophecies. One is the Messiah. One is the Messiah's "forerunner" who prepares the hearts of a remnant of Israel to receive the Messiah's message.

Together they represent the culmination of everything God has been planning, preparing, and pointing to for thousands of years. The Old Testament's "scarlet thread of redemption" runs directly from the Garden of Eden; through the call of Abraham, a man willing to sacrifice his own son; through the Passover sacrifices of unblemished lambs, to the King-Priest David; right to this meeting between Mary of Nazareth and Elizabeth of Hebron.

Mary learned of Elizabeth's advancing pregnancy

during her encounter with Gabriel. It seems Mary
didn't waste any time following up on the angelic
messenger's news, because in the very next verse,
we read:

> Now Mary arose in those days and went into
> the hill country with haste, to a city of Judah,
> and entered the house of Zacharias and greeted
> Elizabeth. (Luke 1:39–40)

Mary must have begun preparing for the one-
hundred-mile journey the very next day. Keep in mind
that Elizabeth is six or seven months farther along than
Mary at this point. We don't know how long it's been
since these two have seen each other. What we do

know is that the moment Mary enters the house and says hello to her relative, something truly extraordinary happens:

> And it happened, when Elizabeth heard the greeting of Mary, that the babe leaped in her womb; and Elizabeth was filled with the Holy Spirit. (Luke 1:41)

It's likely Elizabeth's unborn child, John, was filled with the Spirit at this moment as well. How do we know this? Because one of the things the angel Gabriel told Zacharias beside the altar of incense was that his son would "be filled with the Holy Spirit, even from his mother's womb" (Luke 1:15).

52

Elizabeth experiences something many of the Old Testament prophets experienced. A temporary infilling of the Holy Spirit that inspires her to speak words from God. (That's really all prophecy is—speaking by inspiration of God's Spirit.) Immediately, Elizabeth begins to speak a prophetic word to Mary. She says:

> "Blessed *are* you among women, and blessed *is* the fruit of your womb! But why *is* this *granted* to me, that the mother of my Lord should come to me? For indeed, as soon as the voice of your greeting sounded in my ears, the babe leaped in my womb for joy. Blessed *is* she who believed, for there will be a fulfillment of those things which were told her from the Lord." (Luke 1:42–45)

Three times, in this brief explosion of joy and wonder, Elizabeth uses the word *blessed*. It's the third word of Christmas. But as we're about to discover, as is so often the case, there is more truth in Luke's original Greek than comes through in the English translation.

DAY EIGHT

As we've noted, Elizabeth used the word *blessed* three times in one short prophetic outburst. We twenty-first-century Christians use that word a lot, too.

We bless our food before we eat it. When asked how we're doing, we say, "I'm blessed!" Here in the South, we bless each other's hearts. A lot. A note to Northerners: If someone from my part of the country says "Bless your heart, sweetie" it means one of two things. Either the person has genuine sympathy for your plight, or they think you're sort of clueless. The point is, we throw that word around a great deal.

Elizabeth uses this word under the inspiration of the Holy Spirit. The mere sound of the voice of the woman carrying the only begotten Son of God in her womb is enough to bring the Spirit of God down upon both Elizabeth and her unborn son. In that moment, she becomes aware of Mary's unique condition. Her response is instantaneous:

> Then she spoke out with a loud voice and said, "Blessed *are* you among women, and blessed *is* the fruit of your womb!…Blessed *is* she who believed,

56

for there will be a fulfillment of those things which were told her from the Lord." (Luke 1:42, 45)

What's not apparent in our English Bibles is that Elizabeth uses two very different Greek words here, both of which are translated as "blessed" in most versions of the Bible. This tells us there are two kinds of blessings, and both of them are proclaimed here.

Looking at the original Greek, Elizabeth twice uses the word *eulogeo* in that first sentence above. Speaking of Mary and the unborn Savior, she says "Blessed [*eulogeo*] are you among women…" And speaking of Jesus, she cries out, "and blessed [*eulogeo*] is the fruit of your womb."

You may recognize this Greek word as being the

root of our English word "eulogy," which is basically a speech in which someone says nice things about someone who has passed away. To *eulogeo* does involve speaking, but it is much stronger, much more powerful than that. It describes the power of the *spoken* blessing—a holy act of declaring good and wonderful things over someone, fully believing that those good things will come to pass. This kind of "blessing" requires speaking.

58

The writer of the book of Hebrews uses this word to describe the blessing that Melchizedek spoke over Abraham; and the blessings that Isaac spoke over his sons Jacob and Esau (see Heb. 7:1; 11:20). James uses this word and contrasts it with its extreme opposite—cursing:

With it we bless [*eulogeo*] our God and Father, and with it we curse men, who have been made in the similitude of God. Out of the same mouth proceed blessing [*eulogia*] and cursing. (James 3:9–10)

To speak a curse upon someone is to call for supernaturally bad things to happen to them. To speak a blessing over someone is to call for supernaturally good things for them. And when it's God who speaks a blessing over you, you're *very* blessed indeed. This is what Elizabeth, by inspiration of God's Spirit, is declaring. She is revealing that God has declared wonderful things over Mary and over the boy she carries.

This is a powerful Christmas word for the rest of

59

us, as well. The birth of Jesus Christ was accompanied by declarations of blessing over you and me. In the very next chapter of Luke, angels appear to shepherds near Bethlehem and declare "good tidings of great joy which will be to all people" (Luke 2:10). "All people"! Those same angels spoke a heavenly blessing: "Glory to God in the highest, and on earth peace, goodwill toward men!" (Luke 2:14). That's us, too!

Even so, there is another aspect of being "blessed" hidden in Elizabeth's prophetic word.

60

DAY NINE

After declaring two *eulogeo* blessings—one over Mary and one over the Messiah she carries, Elizabeth ends her prophetic word by declaring:

> Blessed *is* she who believed, for there will be a fulfillment of those things which were told her from the Lord." (Luke 1:45)

The Greek word translated as "blessed" here is a completely different word than the one translated the same way at the beginning of Elizabeth's Holy Spirit–inspired prophecy. Here the word is *makarios* and it simply means "happy." Deeply, profoundly happy. Jesus used this word repeatedly in the portion of His Sermon on the Mount that we call the Beatitudes.

62

There Jesus makes statements like: "Blessed [*makarios*] *are* those who hunger and thirst for righteousness, for they shall be filled" (Matt. 5:6).

Eight consecutive times in this passage Jesus describes a group of people and declares them to be "happy" because, when His kingdom arrives after His death and resurrection, they are going to get what they have desired.

Happiness is an emotion, and the word *makarios* speaks to our emotional well-being. I love the fact that Jesus made these declarations because it reveals that God cares about every part of who we are, including our emotions. This may come as a shock to those who were raised in a grim, harsh religious tradition, but Jesus came to make you happy. It's not the only thing He came to do, but it's certainly part of it. Why? Because God is good and He loves us!

One of Satan's most common deceptions is that if you give your life to Jesus, you'll never be happy again. He sells this lie to people who do not yet know Jesus, whispering, "You like to have fun, don't you? We'll if you follow Jesus, your days of fun will be over!"

What nonsense. I was old enough when I gave my

63

life to Christ to remember what it was like before that day. There was nothing fun about feeling chronically empty, purposeless, self-absorbed, insecure, and filled with shame. It was a miserable way to live. I was anything but *happy*.

Jesus changed all that because that is what He came to do. The third chapter of Acts records Peter delivering one of the very first sermons preached under the New Covenant enacted by Jesus' death and resurrection. In the previous chapter the Holy Spirit was poured out on the day of Pentecost, which makes this one of the first sermons ever preached under the power of the Spirit. Take note of what Peter says here:

64

"To you first, God, having raised up His Servant Jesus, sent Him to bless you, in turning away every one of *you* from your iniquities." (Acts 3:26)

Why did God send Jesus? To bless you! Jesus spoke an extraordinary blessing over you in John 17 (His "High Priestly Prayer"). Your happiness matters to your heavenly Father. Blessed and happy indeed are they who believe.

One synonym for the word *happy* is *merry*. No wonder we wish one another a merry Christmas. *Blessed* is the third word of Christmas.

65

Guidance

"*Arise, take the young Child
and His mother, flee to Egypt,
and stay there until I bring you word;
for Herod will seek the young Child
to destroy Him.*"

MATTHEW 2:13

DAY TEN

Herod the Great, King of Judah—depraved, demented, and paranoid after more than forty years of ruthless rule—has just ordered the deaths of every infant and toddler boy in and around Bethlehem. "Kill them all," is the command.

He aims to end what he perceives to be a threat to his family's hold on the throne. He's heard of some whisperings down in Jerusalem concerning the recent birth of a rightful heir to the throne of David. So, every child under the age of two in the "City of David" must die. We've seen this movie before.

Almost immediately after the fall of man, God made a prophetic promise to undo all the damage that had been done. A "seed" of woman would one day be born and would crush the head of the serpent that had deceived mankind (see Gen. 3:15).

The entire Old Testament can be viewed as a story of God laying the groundwork to bring that promised Savior-Seed into the world; and the enemy's relentless, violent efforts to stop that from happening. Just one battle in that long war came fifteen centuries earlier when another insecure, demonically inspired king,

70

Pharaoh, ordered all the infant boys of the Israelites to be slain.

The enemy of God's people was not able to thwart God's plan back then. And now, having failed to prevent the birth of that "seed," he is making one last, desperate effort to destroy Him. This too, will fail.

An unnamed angel has appeared to Joseph in the night and warned him of the danger to Jesus, the recently born child of his wife, Mary:

> An angel of the Lord appeared to Joseph in a dream, saying, "Arise, take the young Child and His mother, flee to Egypt, and stay there until I bring you word; for Herod will seek the young Child to destroy Him." (Matthew 2:13)

This isn't the first time an angel has given Joseph crucial instructions concerning his role in protecting that "seed" promised all the way back in the Garden of Eden. Nor will it be the last. After learning the girl to whom he was betrothed was with child, Joseph had planned to quietly end their engagement, but an angel had appeared to him in a dream, directing him to continue with the marriage because it was a miracle of God (see Matt. 1:20–21).

After taking his family to refuge in Egypt in response to the angelic warning, Joseph later received another priceless piece of advice:

> Now when Herod was dead, behold, an angel of
> the Lord appeared in a dream to Joseph in Egypt,

saying, "Arise, take the young Child and His mother, and go to the land of Israel, for those who sought the young Child's life are dead." (Matthew 2:19–20)

Scholars are divided over the precise date of Herod's death, but several argue for a date of 1 BC. It's important to note that, because of a medieval mistake in establishing the Gregorian calendar that we still use to this day, Jesus was almost certainly born in either the year 4 BC or 3 BC, according to our current calendar system. This means that at the time of Herod's death, Jesus was probably around three years old.

As Joseph heads back to his ancestral homeland of Judah with his young family, he is visited for a fourth time by an angel in a dream, warning him to avoid Judah, and to settle in the north, in Mary's home of Galilee, instead.

These four events spell out for us the very important, very encouraging fourth word of Christmas—even though this word doesn't explicitly appear in the verses we've examined. We'll explore it next.

DAY ELEVEN

ave you ever gotten lost? I'm talking about becoming truly disoriented and discombobulated as you traveled in a strange place? It's not a good feeling. In fact, it can be downright terrifying. I recall reading a news report in 2019 about a woman who went for a short hike on some trails in Hawaii, got disoriented, and ended up lost in the rain forest for seventeen days.

That's why I'm so glad that one of the seven words of Christmas is *guidance*. No, you won't find that word among the Scriptures we've examined, but it is certainly there as a theme. On four separate occasions, God sent an angel to give vital directions to Joseph, to ensure the safety and well-being of his family. A clear and encouraging message emerging from this part of the Christmas story is that God loves to provide His people with direction and wise instruction—especially in critical moments of our lives.

God has many ways He can deliver that guidance. He frequently uses His Word, the Bible. He'll use other people. He'll speak through the inward voice of the Spirit. Yes, He still speaks prophetically. And, as in Joseph's case, He still speaks through dreams. I recall an especially vivid dream one night that I just knew carried spiritual significance.

In the dream, Debbie and I were driving along and I saw a group of men beating up a guy. I handed her my phone and said, "Call 911." Then I got out of the car and started running toward the men while shouting at them. They ran away at the sound of my voice.

When I reached the man who was being attacked, I saw that he had some sort of mask over his face. I knelt down, cradled the man in my arms, and lifted the mask from his face. I was shocked to see the face of one of my friends. Then, suddenly, I awakened.

I couldn't shake the sense that this unusual dream meant something, so I called my friend the next morning and told him the dream. When I finished,

77

I said, "I think Satan's attacking you right now, and I need you to be honest with me. What's going on?"

After a long pause, he said, "Yes, Robert. To be honest, my marriage is under an all-out assault right now. I just feel like I'm under siege. It's been terrible. Please pray for us." We prayed, and I was also able to point him toward a source of sound, biblical marriage help.

God speaks. God cares. God warns. He guides, instructs, and counsels. The psalmist David understood this. In Psalm 32, he says to God:

> You *are* my hiding place;
> You shall preserve me from trouble;

You shall surround me with songs of
    deliverance. (Psalms 32:7)

God replies, saying:

I will instruct you and teach you in the way
    you should go;
I will guide you with My eye. (Psalms 32:8)

When I think about God's faithfulness to guide
us, I'm also reminded of the familiar and comforting
promise of Proverbs 3:5–6:

Trust in the LORD with all your heart,
And lean not on your own understanding;

In all your ways acknowledge Him,
And He shall direct your paths.

God faithfully guided Joseph. He's promised to direct your paths too, if you'll wholeheartedly put your trust in Him.

80

DAY TWELVE

It's no wonder the psalmist David declared, "The Lord is my Shepherd…He leads me beside still waters." Or that Jesus described Himself as a shepherd, too. God guides! He directs us out of harm's way so we can fulfill His good plans for our lives.

That's the wonderful message that comes through as we read the Christmas story. In fact, we see this truth in places other than just Joseph's dreams. The most obvious example is the "star" that led the Magi directly to Jesus:

> When they heard the king, they departed; and behold, the star which they had seen in the East went before them, till it came and stood over where the young Child was. When they saw the star, they rejoiced with exceedingly great joy. (Matthew 2:9–10)

I suppose it's possible the light in the sky that led these men, road by road, street by street, to the exact house where Joseph, Mary, and Jesus were living was literally some sort of astronomical object. But it's much more likely that this too was an angel. Throughout the

Bible angelic beings are symbolized and portrayed as "stars" in the sky (see Job 38:7; Dan. 8:9; Rev. 1:20).

What's clear is that God intentionally and faithfully led these Magi to the feet of the child Jesus, so they could bestow gifts upon Him. By the way, contrary to all the pageants and nativity scenes we've seen through years, we don't actually know there were three of these sky-watchers from the East who made this journey. The Bible doesn't say how many there were. It only says they brought three types of gifts—gold, frankincense, and myrrh.

Isn't it good to know that God will do whatever is necessary to guide us through the often bewildering jungle called life? You don't have to worry. You don't have to have your precious days filled with anxiety or fear. Why? Because Jesus came. And when He was here, He promised to send the Holy Spirit after He returned to heaven.

Note what Jesus said about the gift of the Spirit:

However, when He, the Spirit of truth, has come, **He will guide you into all truth**; for He will not speak on His own *authority*, but whatever He hears He will speak; and **He will tell you things to come**. (John 16:13; emphasis added)

The Spirit of God will tell you where to go (and warn you where *not* to go). He'll tell you when to move to another city; which job offer to take; and when you should or shouldn't buy something.

84

He's a truly a wonderful, helpful person (the Helper!), and as such, is much, much better than the "star" that led the Magi like a glow-in-the-dark GPS! In fact, you could call part of the ministry of Holy Spirit "Guidance Protection Services" because that's one of the many amazing things He does.

These days most of us are using some form of GPS navigation in our cars that gives us audible, turn-by-turn directions. My wife, Debbie, makes fun of me when we use ours because I frequently forget to pay attention to the instructions. As a result, I miss the turns, and that means the word we hear most is "recalculating." Other times I think I have a better idea than the computer and will ignore her advice. Again, we hear lots and lots of "recalculating."

One time our exasperated GPS said, "Just pull over and let me drive." I'm joking, of course. But it's comforting to know that, even when we make a wrong turn in life, we belong to a God who loves to provide guidance.

Joy

Then the angel said to them,
"Do not be afraid, for behold,
I bring you good tidings of great joy
which will be to all people."

LUKE 2:10

DAY THIRTEEN

*T*idings isn't a word we use much anymore. Even so, most of us know that it basically means "breaking news." And if you're like me, when you see the words *breaking news* scrolling across the bottom of your television screen, you brace yourself for something terrible.

The fact is, people in all times have been more

likely to expect bad news rather than good. Maybe that's why the angels delivering the fifth prophetic word of Christmas to a group of shepherds overseeing a flock of sheep at night felt the need to immediately assure their audience they were about to hear *good* tidings:

90

> Now there were in the same country shepherds living out in the fields, keeping watch over their flock by night. And behold, an angel of the Lord stood before them, and the glory of the Lord shone around them, and they were greatly afraid. Then the angel said to them, "Do not be afraid, for behold, I bring you good tidings of great joy, which will be to all people. (Luke 2:8–10)

You can understand why these shepherds were startled. They're settled in for yet another long, quiet night of guarding the flocks against predators and thieves—one of thousands they've experienced in the past—when suddenly a luminous being appears before them and the entire camp is bathed in shimmering light. It is as if a portal into heaven itself has opened up and the glory of God's throne room is pouring out of it into the dark Judean night. And in a sense, it is.

91

Gabriel's first words to Zacharias had been, "Don't be afraid." Likewise, his second sentence to Mary was, "Do not be afraid." Is this Gabriel again? Very possibly, but the Bible doesn't identify this messenger. What we *do* know is that the angel begins with those very same words of calming reassurance.

They are followed by a reason. He comes bearing wonderful news…news that will bring joy to "all people." The angel's message is, quite literally, "Joy to the World."

Those of us living in the twenty-first century have no way to imagine how dark a place the world was before Jesus entered it—leaving behind a Church that is literally His body and presence, spreading all over the planet like a sweet, life-giving fragrance. We have no idea how saturated with demonic violence, slavery, oppression, suffering, and injustice every nook and cranny of this world was before that baby arrived.

What is this joyful news? "For there is born to you this day in the city of David a Savior, who is Christ the

Lord" (Luke 2:11). In one half of a sentence, we see three key titles attributed to this newborn—"Savior, Christ, and Lord."

This proclamation that will one day bring joy to the world already has heaven rejoicing. No sooner are the words out of the angel's mouth than a vast chorus of angelic praise erupts:

93

> And suddenly there was with the angel a multitude of the heavenly host praising God and saying:
>
> > "Glory to God in the highest,
> > And on earth peace, goodwill
> > toward men!" (Luke 2:13–14)

Here, the fifth word of Christmas has not only been spoken, it has been demonstrated in the rejoicing of angels. Let's explore *joy*.

DAY FOURTEEN

What is this thing called joy…"great joy"…the angel spoke of? And how is it different from the third word of Christmas, *blessed*, which, as we discovered on Day 9 means *happy*?

Happiness is nice. I'd certainly rather have more of it in my life than less. But joy is deeper. Joy is stronger. Joy wells up from the deepest parts of who we are, whereas being happy works its way in from the outside, based on our outward circumstances.

One of the great things about joy is that it doesn't depend on your circumstances. You can have joy in the midst of trouble, even when "happiness" has long since evaporated.

I received an unforgettable lesson about this one Christmas when our kids were still quite young. Right at the threshold the holiday season, we had two unexpected repairs that hit our financial reserves. Our car and a washing machine both failed at the worst possible time.

As a matter of conviction and principle, we've never charged things to credit cards that we couldn't pay off in full at the end of the month. As a result, we were facing what an old Dolly Parton song called a "Hard Candy Christmas." That's a Christmas when the family can't afford to put much more in the kids' stockings than a few pieces of hard candy.

Not surprisingly, that upset me. The father-heart in me was deeply disappointed we seemingly wouldn't be able to bless our children in the way I had planned. I carried that disappointment into my next quiet time with God. I suspect I was carrying some suppressed resentment against God and, as a result, I was just kind of going through the motions.

Our wonderful heavenly Father, who knows us better than we know ourselves, called me on it. I heard His familiar voice say, "Why don't you just go ahead and say it, son?"

"Okay, Father. I'm mad at You."

"I know. *Why* are you mad at Me?"

"Well, because we don't have any money for Christmas, and You obviously don't even care. That's why I'm mad at You."

"So, what does that mean, you 'don't have any money for Christmas'?"

"You know what it means, Lord," I said. "We're not going to be able to have Christmas this year!"

Have you ever said something and regretted it the instant it comes out of your mouth? This was one of those times for me.

Gently but firmly, the Lord's inward voice said:

"Really? You're not going to be able to have Christmas because you don't have money? You're not going to be able to celebrate and rejoice in My Son's birth because of a lack of money? Hmm. So, you're telling Me that your bank balance determines your level of joy. Is that what you're saying, son?"

"Uhhhh…not anymore," I said, making a hasty retreat.

For reasons I will explain in the next devotion, we actually had one of the richest and most meaningful Christmases of our lives that year. Why? Because having Jesus means having deep, abiding joy.

99

DAY FIFTEEN

✳

"Behold, I bring you good tidings of great joy," the angel said (see Luke 2:10).

The Greek word used here is, *chara*. It describes not only the feeling of joy, but also the reason or cause for it. In other words, a *chara* is a joyous thing or event that causes you to experience joy.

Jesus used the word many times throughout His life

and ministry. He used *chara* to describe the celebration that breaks out in heaven when even one sinner repents (see Luke 15:7). He used it to describe what a new mother feels when she holds her baby in her arms for the first time (see John 16:21). Jesus used *chara* not once but twice when speaking to His disciples about the future: "These things I have spoken to you, that My joy may remain in you, and that your joy may be full" (John 15:11).

Genuine joy *remains*. It abides. God sent Jesus to make that kind of joy possible.

In the previous devotion, I mentioned the Christmas in which unexpected expenses sapped our entire budget for gifts. For a moment or two, I allowed my frustration (and pride) to overshadow the deep, abiding joy of knowing Jesus. But the Lord quickly readjusted my perspective.

After I repented for accusing God of being uncaring, I remember saying, "Okay, Father, you know my heart and our circumstances. I want to give my children gifts this Christmas. How are we going to do that?"

The Lord then reminded me that not all gifts are acquired at a store and paid for with money. My mind went to the passages in the Bible that spoke of spiritual gifts. One passage in particular stood out to me. In 1 Timothy 4:14, Paul exhorts his young protégé to not neglect the spiritual gift imparted to him through the laying on of hands.

Suddenly, my imagination was captured by the idea of imparting a different spiritual gift to each of my children through prayer. Debbie and I immediately began praying for guidance to know what gift the Lord wanted to give each of our three children.

As it turned out, God supernaturally provided unexpected income that allowed us to also purchase conventional presents for our kids that year, and we did. But the present Debbie and I were most excited about giving that year was the spiritual kind.

Christmas morning, Debbie and I prayed over each of our kids and asked the Lord to endue and empower them with a specific gift. To this day our kids, now adults with families of their own, will tell you that was one of the most special Christmases in their memories. And they can tell you precisely what spiritual gift they received that morning.

In fact, a couple of weeks later, we got a call from the school. One of my sons' teachers was on the line saying, "Hey, I wanted you to know your kid really caused a stir in class today. I had each student tell the class their favorite gift they'd received over the Christmas vacation. Most of the kids were talking about video games and bicycles. But your son said his dad gave him the gift of leadership!" He was thrilled with his best gift.

I later heard that some of the other students went home and asked their parents, "Why didn't I get the gift of leadership for Christmas?"

Joy is a powerful thing—a source of great strength

that wells up from the deepest parts of our born-again spirits. Once, as I was preparing to officiate a funeral service, the Lord spoke the following truth to me. He said, "Christians are the only people in the world who can grieve and rejoice at the same time." It's true.

When we lose someone dear to us who is a Christian, it's natural to feel a deep sense of loss. Someone familiar and cherished seems to be gone forever. We grieve. But as Paul once wrote, "We do not grieve as those who have no hope" (see 1 Thess. 4:13). We know the separation is only temporary. We'll see them again. That's how joy and mourning can exist side by side.

Jesus made real joy possible. As C. S. Lewis wrote, "Joy is the serious business of heaven."

Redemption

And coming **in** that instant
she gave **thanks** to the Lord,
and **spoke of** Him to all those
who looked for redemption
in Jerusalem.

LUKE 2:10

DAY SIXTEEN

*T*he Temple Mount in Jerusalem has been buzzing with rumors and speculation for more than a month.

The priests and support staff who live and work within the massive complex of Herod's temple have not stopped talking about wild reports that, forty days earlier, some shepherds outside Bethlehem had had an extraordinary encounter with angels. Supposedly, these angels directed them to a nearby newborn infant who is the long-awaited Messiah of Israel.

One of the people pondering the meaning of these amazing reports is a tiny, mysterious holy woman who has been a familiar fixture of temple life for as long as any living person can remember. It is she who will deliver our sixth prophetic word of Christmas. Here is how Luke describes her:

> Now there was one, Anna, a prophetess, the daughter of Phanuel, of the tribe of Asher. She was of a great age, and had lived with a husband seven years from her virginity; and this woman *was* a widow of about eighty-four years, who did not depart from the temple, but served

110

God with fastings and prayers night and day.
(Luke 2:36–37)

There is so much intriguing information in this brief description! First, we learn that Anna's father is named Phanuel. This is actually a form of the Hebrew place name Piniel, which means "face-to-face." It's the name Jacob gave to the place where he met, and wrestled with, God (see Gen. 32:3). Appropriately, Anna is about to meet God face-to-face—in the form of an infant, His only begotten Son.

Secondly, we learn Anna is of the Asher tribe. This is significant because only people of the tribe of Levi are supposed to be living and serving in the temple. Occasionally exceptions were made, however, particularly when an individual clearly was anointed by God as a prophet or prophetess. Here we learn that this is the case with Anna.

Finally, we learn that Anna was of "a great age." In fact, Luke is enough of a gentleman not to state Anna's age directly, but he does give us enough information to do the math. We're told she had been married seven years when her husband died. Then, as a widow, she had served in the temple for eighty-four years. If we assume that she had married at the age of fourteen—the youngest acceptable age for marriage in that culture—she would be at least 105 years old at this time! Of "a great age" indeed.

On this day, the prophetess Anna will deliver the greatest prophetic exclamation of her long life of service to God. A young couple, carrying a forty-day-old infant boy, are making their way up the steps of the temple complex to sacrifice two turtledoves in accordance with the Law of Moses.

DAY SEVENTEEN

*

With short, careful steps, Anna makes her way across the smooth marble surface of the temple's outer court, where Jewish women are allowed to be present. Throughout eighty-four years of service at the Jerusalem temple, this large open plaza outside the gates of the main complex is as close to the heart of the temple she, or any other woman, has ever been permitted to stand.

That heart, the Holy of Holies, is where the very presence of God is believed to dwell. Only the High Priest is allowed into that sacred space, and only once each year. Yet today, this frail, elderly lady is going to get closer to the presence of God than the High Priest ever has. She'll glimpse the face of God in human form.

As she slowly makes her way across the plaza, a commotion near the entrance catches her attention. A gentleman who looks to be even older than she is shouting excitedly, waving his arms, and rejoicing. Standing before the man is a couple with an infant—one of many such couples who arrive each day to sacrifice two birds in order to "redeem" their firstborn—all in accordance with Law of Moses (see Exod. 13:1–16; Lev. 12:8).

Her heart begins to beat faster as the prophetic gift within her whispers the significance of this particular baby boy. She approaches the couple. Luke doesn't provide much detail as to what happens next. He simply says:

> And coming in that instant she gave thanks
> to the Lord, and spoke of Him to all those
> who looked for redemption in Jerusalem.
> (Luke 2:38)

It is no accident that Anna should speak of redemption in this moment. She has met Joseph and Mary who are "redeeming" the One who will one day redeem mankind. Let's explore the word *redemption*.

116

It describes the process of redeeming something or someone. You have to *redeem* to have redemption.

Breaking this down even further, it's important to note that *deem* lies at the root of *redeem*. To deem is to assign value. We say, "What do you deem the value of that property to be?" So, to re-deem is to re-value something, particularly by re-purchasing it. If you buy something, lose it, then buy it back, you've redeemed it.

In this amazing moment in the temple, Anna begins to give thanks and praise to God, because the Spirit has revealed the truth to her. This baby boy is the long-awaited Redeemer of Israel.

Anna knew the Scriptures, including the prophecy of Isaiah 59:20: "The Redeemer will come to Zion, and to those who turn from transgression in Jacob, says the LORD." Zion is the prophetic name of the temple mount in Jerusalem.

So, Anna, after eighty-four years of praying, fasting, and serving in the temple, sees this prophecy fulfilled with her own eyes. The Redeemer has come to Zion.

118

DAY EIGHTEEN

*R*edemption is the overarching theme of the Word of God. When you hold your Bible in your hands, you're holding a redemption story. The greatest of all time, in fact.

By necessity, every redemption story begins with a loss—often through theft or betrayal. This story is no different. On the Bible's opening pages, we see our original ancestors betray the loving Creator who had placed them in charge of a garden, as well as the wider world in which that garden sat. That betrayal results in their selling themselves into slavery.

As a loving Father unfolds His plan to purchase mankind back and restore us to freedom, we repeatedly see types, pictures, and foreshadowings of this redemption narrative on the pages of that story.

120

Isaac is doomed to die as a sacrifice, when at the last minute, God provides a ram as a substitute, effectively buying back the boy's life and freedom. Ruth, rendered destitute in a foreign land by the death of her husband, is rescued from poverty by a "kinsman redeemer" who pays the price that restores her to her husband's land and home.

The Bible overflows with examples of this theme,

but perhaps the most beautiful and striking of these is the story of the prophet Hosea and his unfaithful wife. The entire book of Hosea is essentially the story of a prophet who is asked by God to live out a redemption narrative as a prophetic message to the spiritually unfaithful nation of Israel.

In the first chapter, God directs Hosea to go purchase the freedom of a prostitute and make her his wife. He does so and they have three children together. But eventually she decides to return to her previous life, ultimately becoming a literal sex slave again. Then, in chapter three, God directs Hosea to go and buy her freedom once again, and to restore her as his wife. And he does so (see Hosea 3:1–2). The entire series of events is a powerful prophetic picture at two levels.

First, it shows how God, as Israel's spiritual husband, would eventually pursue and forgive Israel, even though the nation that God had initially redeemed from slavery in Egypt had wandered away into the adultery of idolatry. That unfaithfulness would ultimately lead to the nation of Judah being exiled and held captive in Babylon for seventy years. Even so, God would come and redeem her a second time, and lead her back into the land of promise.

At a higher level, Hosea is prophetically depicting how God sent His own sinless Son as the purchase price to redeem lost, dying humanity back to Himself. What a price He paid. What love and mercy He displayed in buying us back from slavery and sin and death.

122

Jesus once told His disciples, "the Son of Man did not come to be served, but to serve, and to give His life a ransom for many" (Matt. 20:28).

There is a powerful, personal message here for you and me. This story shouts that even when we wander away from God—even when our unfaithfulness puts us in bondage to consequences and curses—our faithful, forgiving Father pursues us with His love. He stands ever willing, ever able to redeem and restore us.

That's what Anna saw prophetically when she looked into the face of a baby in the temple courtyard that day. This is why she testified of it "to all those who looked for redemption in Israel."

Without a doubt, the sixth word of Christmas is *redemption*.

123

Peace

" *Lord, now You are letting*
Your servant depart in peace,
According to Your word;
For my eyes have seen
Your salvation."

LUKE 2:29–30

DAY NINETEEN

Remember the elderly gentleman in the temple courtyard whose excitement and rejoicing got Anna's attention in the previous section? He has a name and a story. He is also the source of our seventh and final prophetic word of Christmas: *peace*.

And behold, there was a man in Jerusalem whose name *was* Simeon, and this man *was* just and devout, waiting for the Consolation of Israel, and the Holy Spirit was upon him. And it had been revealed to him by the Holy Spirit that he would not see death before he had seen the Lord's Christ. (Luke 2:25–26)

The Bible does not specify, but some early church traditions hold that Simeon is 112 years old at this time. This ancient priest had been tenaciously holding on to a precious promise of God for a very long time. He had a word from the Lord that he would not die until he had glimpsed with his own eyes, the "Lord's Christ," the Messiah.

Luke also tells us that Simeon had long been waiting for "the Consolation of Israel." This is an interesting phrase.

The Greek word translated as "consolation" here is *paraklesis*—and it means "to bring comfort or solace." Paul used this same word in Philippians 2:1 when he wrote: "Is there any encouragement from belonging to Christ? Any comfort from his love?" (NLT). You may have also noticed the similarity to the word *paraclete*, which many believers know is one of the ways Jesus referred to the Holy Spirit, and is usually translated "Helper" or "Comforter."

129

Given the way Luke uses it, the phrase "Consolation of Israel" had clearly become a familiar one among the Jews living under the iron heel of Roman rule. It's rooted in the opening words of Isaiah 40—a passage that every first-century Jew knew to be a prophecy concerning the Messiah:

"Comfort, yes, comfort My people!"
Says your God.
"Speak comfort to Jerusalem, and cry out to her,
That her warfare is ended,
That her iniquity is pardoned." (Isaiah 40:1–2)

Now, Isaiah was originally written in Hebrew, but most Jewish people in Jesus' day were more familiar with a Greek version of the Old Testament called the Septuagint. Would you like to know what Greek word the Septuagint uses twice in Isaiah 40:1? It's the related word, *parakleos*! This reveals what Luke meant in saying that Simeon and others were looking for "the Consolation of Israel." They were looking for the one who would bring comfort, peace, and pardon to

the downtrodden, discouraged, despairing people
of God.

Why is Simeon there to greet Mary and Joseph
at the precise moment they are entering the temple
courtyard? Because the Spirit of God told him to
go. Now!

So he came **by the Spirit** into the temple. And
when the parents brought in the Child Jesus, to do
for Him according to the custom of the law, he took
Him up in his arms and blessed God and said:

"Lord, now You are letting Your servant
    depart in peace,
According to Your word;

For my eyes have seen Your salvation
Which You have prepared before the face of
    all peoples,
A light to *bring* revelation to the Gentiles,
And the glory of Your people Israel."
    (Luke 2:27–32; emphasis added)

Simeon has finally laid his dimming, aged eyes upon the source of all consolation and comfort. He can now depart "in peace."

DAY TWENTY

Simeon was clearly a man with a close relationship with the Holy Spirit. He had received and held tightly to a word from the Lord about seeing the Messiah in his lifetime. And he'd been sensitive to a prompting from the Spirit to go to the temple, arriving at the precise moment the promised Messiah was entering the building.

Now, in this moment of joy, he delivers a prophecy

to Mary, the mother. This word, however, is not all happy news. Yet every word is true:

> Then Simeon blessed them, and said to Mary His mother, "Behold, this *Child* is destined for the fall and rising of many in Israel, and for a sign which will be spoken against (yes, a sword will pierce through your own soul also), that the thoughts of many hearts may be revealed." (Luke 2:34–35)

Here Simeon sees something about the role of the Messiah and many other scholars of that time had missed. Jesus wasn't going to unite all the Jews in opposition to Rome. On the contrary, He was called and destined to divide them. For some He would be

134

"the Way" to salvation. For many others, He would become a "stone of stumbling" leading to destruction (see Matt. 21:42–44). Disagreements over who Jesus was would soon divide families (see Luke 12:53).

Simeon prophetically sees that how people respond to the good news about Jesus will determine whether they "rise" or "fall."

Jesus will be a "sign, which will be spoken against," he declares. Indeed, throughout His ministry Jesus performed countless signs. And true to Simeon's prophecy, many in the religious leadership of the nation spoke against Him. Just as Simeon prophesied, the way people respond to Jesus' words and ministry will reveal their hearts.

For any Jew of this day, this is obviously painful

135

news to hear about the long-awaited, eagerly anticipated Messiah of Israel. But the news is even worse for mother Mary. "Yes, a sword will pierce through your own soul," he tells her.

With the benefit of hindsight, we know that every word was true. Jesus was rejected by many of the people He came to deliver. He did expose the hearts of the hateful, the prideful, and the hypocritical. And Mary was there when they ultimately called for Jesus to be killed because of it.

We know that Mary was there when the Roman soldier's spear ended her son's life. Just moments earlier, Jesus had looked down from the cross and arranged for her care. This startling prophetic word about the Prince of Peace lets Mary know that the road ahead would not be all roses. Some thorns were in her future.

That's true for all of us. Life brings painful, difficult moments. Storms come to every house. Yet, because the Prince of Peace came, we can experience peace in the midst of the fiercest storms of life.

My family has a new appreciation for that fact these days. Back in 2018, I came astonishingly close to dying. Two of my arteries tore and I lost over half of the blood in my body in just a few short hours. My wife had to hear the paramedics say that my blood pressure was too low to register, and that they could not find a pulse.

She had to hear them say that if there was anything she wanted to say to me, she should say it quickly.

She had to hold up her phone to take a video while I expressed my love for my children. She had to watch the CareFlight helicopter take off, not knowing if we had just spoken for the last time. It was a nightmarish night for my sweet wife.

Obviously, our faithful God kept me around. But in the aftermath, Debbie has been asked many times how she felt when it seemed that I was at death's door. On scores of occasions she's been asked how she handled it. Each time her answer has remained the same. She says, "I was concerned, but I had a supernatural peace."

Debbie understands what Paul was talking about when he wrote:

138

Then you will experience God's peace, which exceeds anything we can understand. His peace will guard your hearts and minds as you live in Christ Jesus. (Philippians 4:7 NLT)

Jesus came to give us supernatural peace.

139

DAY TWENTY-ONE

*H*aving finally glimpsed Israel's Messiah, a joyful Simeon announced that he could "depart in peace." *Peace* is a word that permeates the Christmas story.

When Zacharias, filled with the Holy Spirit, began to prophesy on the day of his miracle son's circumcision, he closed his long prophetic message by declaring that the Messiah was coming "To guide our feet into the way of peace" (Luke 1:79). The angelic announcement to the shepherds included the prophetic blessing, "peace on earth." In Isaiah's prophecy about the coming Messiah who would be born of a virgin, we learn that one of His names will be Prince of Peace (see Isaiah 9:6).

That's the amazing thing about these seven words of Christmas, they all interconnect and overlap. Several of the prophecies talked about redemption. Simeon's prophecy mentioned salvation. Several mention blessing or being blessed. Most of them produce joy in the speaker or the hearers. Taken together, these seven words are the true heart of the Christmas story because they represent the heart of God for you and me.

Something else strikes me when I step back and

look at these stories as a whole. Those involved in giving and receiving these words are a remarkably diverse group. The fact that Anna was at least 105 and Simeon was 112 tells me that no one is ever too old to be used by God. And that Mary was but a teenage girl from a small country town reveals that you're never too young or uncredentialed to be God's instrument to change the world.

142

Some of these words were given by angels but some came through ordinary people just like you and me. Some came to individuals like Mary and Joseph, but others came to groups like the shepherds. Of those six individuals, three were men (Zacharias, Joseph, and Simeon) and three were women (Anna, Mary, and Elizabeth).

What does this tell us? That God is no respecter
of persons! There is no discrimination under the rule
of King Jesus. No elite level for certain groups only.
In fact, the Word says that in Christ, there is no such
thing as male or female, Jew or Gentile. Rich and poor;
city and country; those with multiple academic degrees
and those who have only graduated from the school of
hard knocks—all can receive words from God. All can
deliver words from God, too. The ground truly is level
at the foot of the cross.

143

All this is possible only because Jesus came. He
came to set right everything in the world that got
twisted and broken in the Fall. He came to reconcile us
to God. He came to calm the raging storms of fear and
shame in our souls. He came to bring us *peace*. So…

And let the peace that comes from Christ rule in your hearts. For as members of one body you are called to live in peace. And always be thankful. (Colossians 3:15, NLT)

CONCLUSION

*M*y prayer is that as you journeyed through the pages of this book, you found a deeper appreciation for the extraordinary Savior whose birth we celebrate at Christmas. He is more wonderful than we know, or even can know.

I hope you understand that He is a perfect representation of the nature and character of our Father God. Jesus literally showed us what God is like—His character, His compassion, His ways. And in coming to earth as one of us, Jesus showed us how much God loves us.

Before you set this book aside, I'd like to ask you to take a moment to just quiet your mind and soul. Then ask the Holy Spirit a simple question: "What are you saying to me through this book?" Perhaps the Spirit of God will highlight one or more of these words of Christmas that you need in your life right now.

Salvation

Favor

Blessed

Guidance

Joy

Redemption

Peace

Do you need guidance? Do you need joy? Do you need peace? Jesus came to be all of these things to you and through you. He's available and willing. Just press into Him. There is never a better time than Christmas to receive the gifts Jesus came to bring you.

I have a wonderful word for you in this holy moment. His name is Jesus.

ABOUT THE AUTHOR

obert Morris is the founding lead senior
pastor of Gateway Church, a multicampus
church based out of the Dallas–Fort Worth Metroplex.
Since it began in 2000, the church has grown to more
than 71,000 active attendees. His television program
airs in over 190 countries, and his radio program,
Worship & the Word with Pastor Robert, airs in more
than 1,800 radio markets across America. He serves

as chancellor of The King's University and is the bestselling author of numerous books, including *The Blessed Life*, *Frequency*, *Beyond Blessed*, and *Take the Day Off*. Robert and his wife, Debbie, have been married forty years and are blessed with one married daughter, two married sons, and nine grandchildren.